PICTURE LIBRARY
STUNT RIDING

PICTURE LIBRARY
STUNT RIDING

Norman Barrett

Franklin Watts

London   New York   Sydney   Toronto

Safety Warning
The stunts featured in this book were performed by professionals or by riders and teams who practised under professional controls. Under no circumstances should any of these stunts or tricks be attempted by inexperienced riders except under expert supervision.

© 1987 Franklin Watts Ltd

First published in Great Britain
  1987 by
Franklin Watts Ltd
12a Golden Square
London WIR 4BA

First published in the USA by
Franklin Watts Inc
387 Park Avenue South
New York
N.Y. 10016

First published in Australia by
Franklin Watts
14 Mars Road
Lane Cove
2066 NSW

UK ISBN: 0 86313 493 9
US ISBN: 0-531-10276-9
Library of Congress Catalog Card Number 86-50642

Printed in Italy

Designed by
Barrett & Willard

Photographs by
"A" Team
Action Plus
N.S. Barrett
Chiltern Studios/Bedford Trucks
Colorsport
Daubney Variety
Demoniam
T.B. Phillips
Rex Features
Royal Artillery
The Royal Signals White Helmets
Spirit of Britain
Stuntarama
Andy Willsheer

Illustration by
Rhoda and Robert Burns

Technical Consultants
Officer Commanding, The White Helmets
Roy Pratt, Honda Imps
Shirley Tarrant, Spirit of Britain

Contents

Introduction	6
The big leap	8
Display teams	10
Stunts	16
Daredevil riders	21
Other stunt machines	23
The story of stunt riding	28
Facts and records	30
Glossary	31
Index	32

The big leap

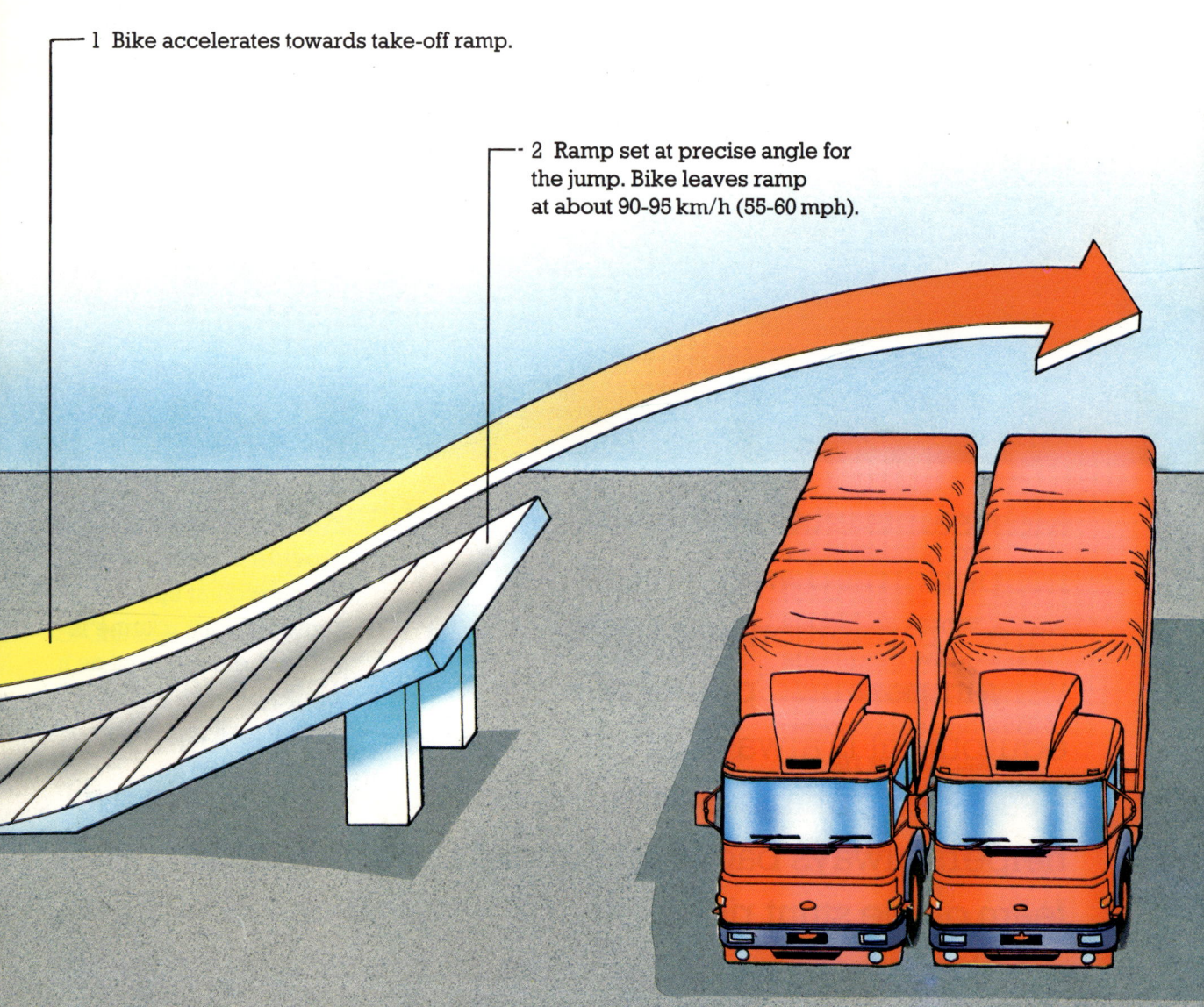

1 Bike accelerates towards take-off ramp.

2 Ramp set at precise angle for the jump. Bike leaves ramp at about 90-95 km/h (55-60 mph).

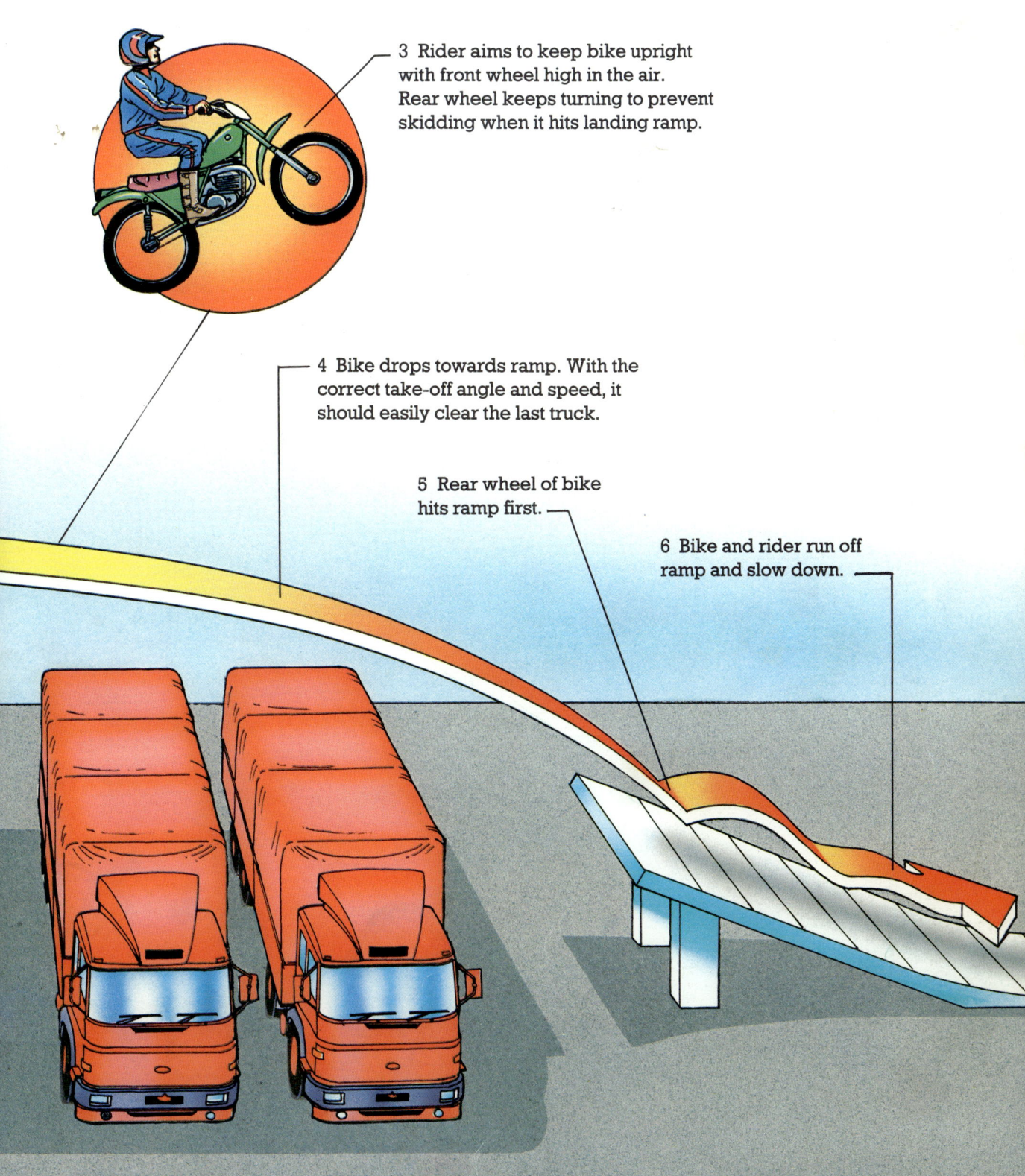

3 Rider aims to keep bike upright with front wheel high in the air. Rear wheel keeps turning to prevent skidding when it hits landing ramp.

4 Bike drops towards ramp. With the correct take-off angle and speed, it should easily clear the last truck.

5 Rear wheel of bike hits ramp first.

6 Bike and rider run off ramp and slow down.

Display teams

Some of the best and most famous display teams are made up of military riders. They are highly trained regular soldiers rather than special stuntmen.

There are also special stunt teams who make their living by putting on shows. Junior groups are also organized, with some members as young as six years old.

▷ The driver is an adult, but the other riders are all juniors, members of the Honda Imps display team. With the aid of a ladder and special harnesses, they are performing a balance called "Blooms".

▽ Four members of the White Helmets perform a simple but graceful balance on one bike.

▷ A perfect pyramid of 15 people progresses smoothly along a racing circuit to entertain the crowd.

Mounting a pyramid, or a fan, as it is known to the riders, calls for balance, skill and, above all, teamwork.

The Royal Artillery team in the picture have built up their pyramid with the help of footrests on all the bikes, a frame attached to the middle bike and harnesses worn by the row of three riders.

△ Harnesses are used for performing this graceful balance. At low speeds, the driver must constantly make small adjustments in order to keep the bike going and on course.

◁ This classic pose is called a "Double Jimmy".

14

In team displays, the drivers have special responsibilities. They must keep their bikes in perfect working order, and have them tuned perfectly before the start of a show.

With tricks and balances performed at slow speed, the most difficult part is to keep the bike going. This calls for precision riding, or the engine may cut out.

▽ In some stunt teams, the motorcycle riders may be required to mount another kind of vehicle. Fortunately, they are accustomed to balancing on two-wheeled machines!

◁ The "Bucking Bronco", a front-wheel wheelie.

▷ For a 6-year-old rider, jumping through a paper hoop is the first step to more exciting stunts.

▽ Riding through a "Hoop of Fire". Special fire-resistant clothing must be worn and helpers must be ready with fire extinguishers.

19

◁ A stuntman rides across a tightrope, while a graceful acrobat helps to balance this tricky stunt from below.

▽ The American daredevil stuntman Evel Knievel soars over a line of buses at Wembley Stadium on a tour of Britain.

Other stunt machines

Stunt riding on BMX bikes, called freestyle, has become very popular, and these are ideal machines for youngsters to practise on. As with motorbikes, however, safety is important and helmets must be worn.

Cars and trucks are not as manoeuvrable as bikes, but some drivers perform remarkable stunts.

△ Freestyle BMXers can perform spectacular tricks called "aerials" off "quarter-pipes", or curved ramps.

▷ A truly remarkable demonstration of two-wheel driving. Jacques Bataille, a member of a family of French stunt drivers, has just set this heavy truck on two wheels by means of a ramp, which can be seen in the background.

He then proceeded to give a motor racing crowd an exhibition by driving a complete lap of the racing circuit on two wheels. This was a distance of about 3 km (nearly 2 miles), with tight curves and hairpin bends.